Who['s in] Charge of Your Life?

A Personal Guide to
the Principles of
Accomplishment

Brian Martin and Peter Loeffen

REED

Contact Details
IAS Learning Group Ltd,
Private Bag 300 178,
249 Wright Road,
Albany, New Zealand.

Ph (64) 09 415 7561
Fax (64) 09 415 7564
Email: ias@iprolink.co.nz

Published by Reed Books, a division of Reed Publishing (NZ) Ltd, 39 Rawene Rd, Birkenhead, Auckland. Associated companies, branches and representatives throughout the world. Website: www.reed.co.nz

© 1999 Brian Martin and Peter Loeffen
The authors assert their moral rights in the work.
IAS — Ideas, Action, Success

ISBN 0 7900 0687 1
First published 1999

Edited by Carolyn Lagahetau

Printed in New Zealand

We dedicate this book to the children of New Zealand.

Acknowledgements

The authors gratefully acknowledge the ideas, help, support and encouragement that they have received from the many people who have helped to make this book possible. In particular, we'd like to thank and acknowledge the following people:

Alexander Everitt of Oregon, USA, pioneer of transformational leadership and known as the teacher of teachers, for making his work and teaching available for all and anyone who wanted it, which he gave as a gift.

Robert White of Denver, USA, principal of ARC Associates, for bringing the learning to Brian through his Vision Quest programme, and for his inspiring vision of 'One World, One People'.

Dr Ray Blanchard of Oregon, USA, a true transformational facilitator and the principal creator of the original learning programmes for IAS, for inspiring Brian, Pete and the many graduates of Genesis who have had the good fortune of experiencing his outstanding facilitation first-hand.

Napoleon Hill, whose book *Think and Grow Rich* has influenced Brian from a young age.

Gillian Chater, founding team member of IAS, co-creator and principal architect of today's IAS programmes, for her commitment and dedication in bringing this learning to the business community of New Zealand.

The staff and facilitators of IAS, for their commitment and for their excellent delivery of the learning through the IAS programmes.

Brian's wife Keiko, for her tremendous support to Brian and her patience and guidance in keeping him on track, and Brian's two sons Michael and Robert for their ongoing encouragement and their pride in his work.

Pete's wife Pam, for supporting and encouraging Pete to pursue his visions, and Pete's son Eddie and daughter Kimberley for sharing their dad so he could write this book.

Tom Tusher, former USA and International President of Levi Strauss & Co., who hired Brian as Country Manager of Levi's New Zealand, for his mentoring and friendship, and his ability to get Brian to push the boundaries.

Robert T. Grohman, a czar of business, a role model, and a former USA and International President of Levi Strauss & Co., for his mentoring and friendship, and for giving Brian his first opportunity to be an international businessman.

Günther Speisshofer, President and owner of Triumph International, the world's largest underwear makers, an entrepreneur, visionary and pioneer of international business, for the trust he gave Brian in running Triumph's business in Japan, and for inspiring Brian with his entrepreneurial ability to be creative and take risks.

The special group of people whose stories are sprinkled throughout the book, for their courage and openness in sharing their personal experiences with us and for showing us the learning in action.

And most importantly, the thousands of graduates of the IAS learning programmes, for their courage and inspiration, and for the privilege of being able to pass on the learning to them, and especially for the extraordinary and outstanding things that they've achieved in their lives from the IAS programmes.

Contents

Introduction

When we announced to our friends and colleagues that we were going to write a book, they asked us, not surprisingly, 'What's it going to be about?' When we said, 'It's about helping people to be more effective leaders of their own lives', they got very interested. 'When will it be ready?' they demanded. 'I want a copy signed by the authors!' they proclaimed. 'I'll proofread it for you!' they offered. We seemed to have touched on a very common need: people searching for ways to get their personal and professional lives on to a more effective track. Naturally, we were delighted at the interest the book generated before it was even written!

So how did the book come about? Well, in working with many people over many years, we've seen for ourselves again and again that people forge their own success, and we've come to understand how they do that. Throughout the years we've used this understanding to help people discover how to achieve their own success, both personally and professionally. And from working with organisations, we've also come to understand that it's people being the best they can be, both personally and professionally, which is the key to organisational success.

In writing this book we can now bring our understanding to many more people, who in turn can extend the learning to their colleagues, friends, families and organisations. Business people can use the learning in this book to help them advance their careers and become leaders of their own personal and professional lives. Others can use it to help them find and achieve their purpose in life, whatever it may be.

Who's in Charge of Your Life?

What is it that's brought you to this book? Perhaps you're interested in getting your life, career or current job more on to the track you'd like it to be on. Perhaps you'd like to become more effective personally or professionally. Or maybe you're simply trying to discover your major purpose in life.

Whatever your reason, this book is designed to help you find and get yourself on to the path that you really want to be on, and to succeed in accomplishing the outcomes you want. We begin by opening your awareness about yourself and what you want to accomplish. We then guide you through a process that will help you develop the vision, understanding and skills to accomplish the outcomes you want. And along the way, we help you understand yourself and others better, show you how to recognise and overcome the traps that stand in your way, and how to make better choices as events unfold.

Throughout the book you'll also find some personal views from some of the people we've worked with over the years, people around New Zealand who are right now using the learning captured in this book to accomplish the outcomes they want.

What we want is for you to build the learning from the book into your personal and business life, and use it to fully succeed in your chosen endeavours. We believe that all of us have the possibility to do this, and that to succeed we need only a clear and definite purpose, a compelling vision, and attention to the principles of accomplishment. If this book helps you achieve that for yourself, then our purpose in writing it has been fulfilled.

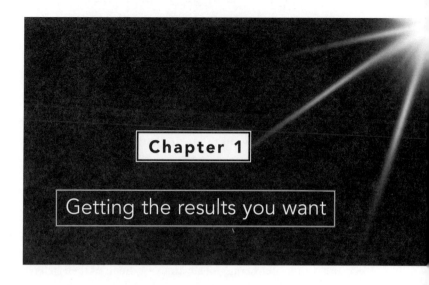

Chapter 1

Getting the results you want

As each minute ticks by on the great cosmic clock, your life 'happens'. Minute by minute your life streams by. The future turns into the present, and recedes forever into the past.

You could, if you wanted to, be a virtual bystander in your life, and by and large it would 'happen' anyway, progressing to its natural end anyway, as the clock ticked on. You might be surprised at how many people live their lives in more or less that fashion. Perhaps there's an element of that in all of us.

Much stronger though, is the basic human drive to self-determination, to exercise some control over how our lives unfold. And in this drive lie the seeds of a lifelong struggle, as we put our energy and focus into achieving the outcomes we want for our lives.

However, as you've no doubt experienced, getting the results you want is no simple task. The fact is, many events will occur along the way over which you have little or no control. These events are neither 'for' nor 'against' you. They're neutral, and as such they 'don't care' about you and your desires.

Who's in Charge of Your Life?

What this means in practice is that it's unlikely that events will happen to align with the results you want. For you to get the results you want in your life requires your energy and focus. This may sound selfish, but not if you express what you want in terms of what you want to *give* to the world with your life.

As you might expect, some of the approaches you take to getting the results you want will work better than others. In fact, your entire accomplishment may well rest on the approaches you take. It makes sense then to put some attention into learning which approaches work well and which ones to avoid. Because people aren't consciously aware of much of their behaviour, in our experience, it's common to find people using approaches that actually hinder their pursuit of the outcomes they really want to accomplish.

With some understanding of the principles of accomplishment and the mind traps that block accomplishment, you can largely avoid these problems. More importantly though, this understanding can strongly develop your capability to accomplish the outcomes you want, whether in a business project or in your life overall. The net effect is to make it much more likely that you'll get the results you want, and that you'll do so faster and more easily.

When I learnt the principles of accomplishment, I discovered that what I thought were the primary drivers for me simply weren't, and I saw that many of my frustrations were common in others too. But I also learnt that I should and can control my own destiny. — J.

In this book, our focus is on the approaches you take rather than the actions undertaken. We focus on you as the key person in getting the results you want. We focus your attention on to your understanding of yourself and what you want to accomplish. We take you on a structured walk through the principles of accomplishment, and explore one by one the key mind traps that block accomplishment. We explore the approaches you take to get other people's help, and your behaviours in dealing with those people. We focus on the multiple roles you'll play as the leader ultimately responsible for getting the results you want, and finally we look at how you handle your own success when you 'arrive'.

Are you ready for this intense focus on yourself? If so, then start by answering this question: What do you really want to accomplish?

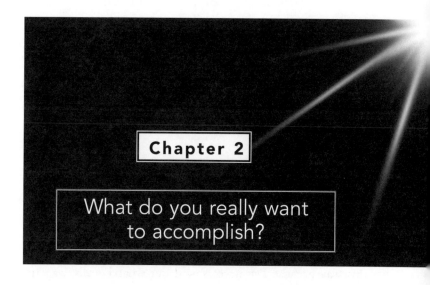

Chapter 2

What do you really want to accomplish?

Do you know what you really want to accomplish in your life-time? If not, you're not alone. Many people don't. It's not something people dwell on. Maybe there's an occasional nagging feeling that one really ought to get this sorted out, but for many of us the issue just doesn't get to the top of our daily To Do list. So we never really get stuck in and work it out. Anyway, why should we? We've got by all right so far, haven't we?

Well, … maybe. But consider this: a very common theme we notice in the people we meet through our work is a definite feeling that the track their life is on is not altogether the track they'd like it to be on. And guess what? There's also a common theme that this isn't a new feeling. It's been growing slowly but steadily for years. Most of these people are business managers, so they're typically over 30, and they've been around for a while and have more than a few clues, but still they're looking. As we noted in the introduction, there's a real thirst for a coherent way for these folk to get their personal and professional lives on to a more effective track.

Who's in Charge of Your Life?

I was tired enough of the way I was and the way I worked to be open to a new way. I was successful, and yet in my heart the success was a trapping. It wasn't deep. There was a dimension missing. — B.

Interestingly, although in retrospect it's pretty obvious, people don't tend to make the connection that leads to the answer. Sure, they feel that their lives or their careers aren't on the track they'd like. But, perhaps because the feeling grows so slowly, they just don't seem to have the flash of insight that says, 'I feel this way because I've never sorted out what I really want to accomplish in my lifetime.'

When you feel your life or career isn't altogether on the track you'd like it to be on, it's very likely that you're in that situation because you haven't mapped out exactly what track you do want to be on. And the bad news is that you're likely to remain stuck there until you work it out. Makes sense really, doesn't it?

Well, you say, I'll just work it out then, and off I'll go! Actually, it's almost that straightforward, but it's not as easy as it sounds to actually do, and that's where the rest of this book comes in, to help you achieve this simple but elusive task. So let's begin!

In today's complex world, people are finding it harder and harder to know what they really want. This is natural, because change is getting faster and faster, and also because it's very unlikely that you can define what you want as a single thing. It's much more likely that what you want is a mixture of things. You want to accomplish things in your career, your relationships, financially, where you live, your health, your sport, all sorts of things.

What do you really want to accomplish?

Of course it would be wonderful if all of these wants could be achieved together, but here comes a key problem: often these wants are in conflict with each other. You want to achieve a sports goal, but practice is needed, and that takes time, and you also need that time to achieve what you want from studying, or working, or being with your family, or all of these and more.

With a positive outlook this leads to a balancing act, with the result that everything makes room for everything else, and none of your wants is really fully satisfied, although most or all of them can be achieved to at least some extent. With a not-so-positive outlook, the conflicting wants lead to frustration, a feeling of constraint, and 'I want to, but I can't', or 'I don't want to, but I have to.'

How many of us live our lives more or less like this? It seems that even the smartest of us often struggle to get past this problem. The net result is that many people, when asked, 'Are you accomplishing what you want in life?', are less than sure. Press them, and you can almost see their mental gears whirring, as they search uncertainly for an answer. In fact, they're searching for two answers. They first need to reflect on what they want in life, and they then need to assess the extent to which they're accomplishing it.

In our experience, most come unstuck on the first part; they're not all that sure about what they want to accomplish in life overall. Their many conflicting wants have resulted in there being no overall answer in their minds. Why is this? If you explore this with people, as we have, you find the main reason is that they've never made a distinction in their minds between what they want and what they really love and truly desire. This is a key distinction, because 'want' comes from a feeling of lack, whereas love and desire lead to passion and energy to create and to take risks. We'll explore this more later.

The second part is no easier. When people know that they're compromising on many of their wants, they're no longer clear about the extent to which they're accomplishing what they want overall.

We see this pattern in people all the time. For us, it would be nice if this problem could be solved at this level. But it makes sense, doesn't it, that if you don't really know what you want to accomplish in life, then you don't really know what your life is about, and so you don't really know yourself very well at a fundamental level. So it's at this level that the solution lies, and later on we'll discuss this further as well.

First though, let's look at some answers from people who do know what they want in life. To begin with, we've noticed that these people have usually thought about their lives in total, not just to date. Have you? This simple move brings many benefits, and is surprisingly straightforward to do. If you haven't already done it, here's a useful method.

A good way to start is to close your eyes and ask yourself how old you plan to be when you die. This may seem absurd at first, but there's good evidence that people choose when they will die. What do you imagine people would answer when asked this? Would you expect people to have high ambitions, to want to live for ever? Do you want that? We've asked many people this question, and the range of answers is quite broad, but typically they range from 'I'll be happy to reach 70' to 'Well, I want to get to over 100 at least.'

What do you really want to accomplish?

> *Why do some of us short-change ourselves by settling for 70? You'll see some of the reasons as you read on, but for now, consider how fundamental your lifespan is to what you want to achieve in life.*

An interesting point here is that quite a few of the people who aim 'low' with their lifespan defend this by arguing that their quality of life will 'not be worth it' over their target age. This raises the whole question of how to lead your life in such a way that you end up in the sizeable group of elderly people whose quality of life is just fine, thank you. And that in turn raises the question of the extent to which your quality of life in your later years is something you can influence yourself. Again, the 'low aimers' typically feel that they have little or no say in how good their later lives will be, and fear the worst, but there are many people who know otherwise, and there is strong evidence to support them. We don't plan to delve into this discussion here, but there's some suggested reading[1] on this point at the end of the book that should convince even the hardiest of doubters.

So, whatever age you plan to die, close your eyes and imagine yourself now at that age. Imagine that you're about to die. Take your time, and be real about it — it's important. In your final minutes, what will you think about? Not surprisingly, most people we've asked say they'd reflect on how their lives had been, and what they'd accomplished. If that was you, and you asked yourself, 'Am I satisfied that I've accomplished what I wanted in life?', what would your answer be?

Imagine that your answer to this question turns out to be 'Yes'. Yes, you have accomplished what you wanted to in your life. What a fulfilling moment that would be! Now here's the key question: what things, in your imagination, had you done with your life that enabled you to say that you'd accomplished what you wanted? Answer that, and you'll be able to see what the rest of your life needs to be about.

We've helped many people do this, and the results have been very positive. So reflect and imagine for a while, and remember to listen to your heart, and not just your head. A word of caution though. It's not uncommon for people to envision what they want in terms of what they want to get from their lives. For example, 'I want to own a house, a yacht, travel, see places, meet people', and so on. However, these are 'false' answers, like fool's gold. Why? Consider the following.

There's a learning game you can play in a group, called the lifeboat exercise. In this exercise, people in a group pretend that their boat is sinking and there is room for just a few on a lifeboat, while the rest will perish. Taken seriously, it's a grim situation. To decide who will go on the lifeboat, each person says why they should go, then each of them votes for who will actually go.

From running this game many times, we've seen that people's votes are based on their perception of how much the world needs them, in other words what they will give to the world, not what they'll take from it. Interestingly, and very important-ly, natural 'givers' know that their giving brings them far more in return than if they had set out to 'take' in the first place.

If you doubt this, consider what their giving has already brought them: their life in the form of a precious place on the lifeboat! Note very well that such giving is not about sacrifice.

What do you really want to accomplish?

Rather, it's about making a contribution and giving personal value.

The lifeboat exercise really focused my mind on the approach I was taking. I was a bystander rather than a participant — a taker rather than a giver — that was a real shock. — J.

So, back to the last day of your life. We propose that the real answer lies in the field of what you will give, rather than what you will get. Where have you been coming from, giving or taking? In our experience, the number of people who are clear about what they want to accomplish with their life, expressed as what they want to *give*, is fairly small, but these are the truly successful ones. Think of this as a very big clue!

Once again, envision for a while. What will you have given with your life when you die?

Of course, from this process you might still end up with a number of things you want to accomplish, each of which is inevitably in conflict with the other things vying for your precious time. In our experience, having multiple competing wants strongly detracts from your sense of accomplishment and, very importantly, from your actual forward progress. It's hard to effectively move the ball down the field when you hold conflicting views about where 'down the field' actually is! If you look inside yourself, you may well recognise this conflict and the dissipating effect it's having on your sense of life being on the track you want it on.

By contrast, in our experience, truly successful people have resolved in their mind and heart their real purpose in life, their driving force, their motivation, and they are truly committed to that purpose. The power such clarity and commitment brings you has to be experienced to be believed, but it is impressive! We simply can't overstate the importance of this clarity and commitment. If you truly desire to do one single thing that will put your life on the track you want it to be on, then find your real purpose in life, and wholeheartedly commit yourself to it.

When your real purpose is clear, you'll find that all the competing wants underneath it simply fall into place quite naturally, and that is a very valuable thing to have happen. And just as importantly, you'll find that you no longer feel the need to move away from the things you don't want. You'll simply move towards what you really desire, and that will settle that. Think of this as another big clue!

There are several ways you can do this. There's a good chance that you can identify your real purpose by understanding what you must accomplish to feel fulfilled on the last day of your life. A good place to start looking is to consider which of your competing wants you're truly passionate about. It helps if you write down your wants as a list — why not do that now? Imagine yourself in a situation where your list of wants has to be given up, one by one. What would your priorities be? Which of your wants would you let go first, and which ones would you simply never let go? Is there a key theme running through your list? Understand that theme, and you may have it.

As you can see, getting your life on to the track you want it on is not a matter of chance, luck or wishful thinking. As those who have done it can attest, you need to make a concerted effort to discover your real purpose. Of course if you have no clear idea of how to go about that, then you may never work it out. But, armed with the tools we've given you so far and the rest of the book still to come, you're in a pretty good position to discover your real purpose and commit yourself wholeheartedly to it. That's provided, of course, that you really want to. Do you? Are you genuinely willing to put in the personal energy and take the personal risks needed to discover your real purpose? How ready are you, really? One thing is sure: if you're not ready and willing, then us helping you counts for little.

We'd like to make a crucial point here. The power to put your life on to the track you truly desire comes from finding and committing yourself to your real purpose, however easy or hard it might be to do that. If you truly desire to achieve that, you will keep up the pursuit no matter how hard it gets. It might require you to face up to yourself warts and all, and finally get to know yourself and who you really are. Draw strength from knowing that many people have gone before you on this quest, and they have succeeded. So can you. But for each of us, as always in life, 'if it's to be, it's up to me'. You are the only one who can create your own results and your own reality. It's your choice. Seek yourself and grow; avoid yourself and get stuck.

I hadn't been used to not winning. I very nearly quit at that point — I didn't want to be that challenged. — J.

This is a tough step for some, but it's crucial. Yes, there can be pain, but we've found that the benefits are so great that people who have successfully passed this point have no regrets, just the joy of true self-discovery. It's like a parachute jump — trepidation before, exhilaration after!

Who's in Charge of Your Life?

Let's now return to some of the deeper questions: what is your life about? And just who are you anyway?

Why are these questions important? Simply put, it's because the deeper levels are powerful determinants of what happens on the surface. It follows that you can get amazing power from understanding yourself at the deeper levels and using that understanding to align yourself better to your real purpose.

Even so, is this really necessary? In our view, yes, because the opposite is also true — you lose an amazing amount of power when you don't understand yourself at the deeper levels. And that lost power is one of the principal reasons that most people are stuck in the state of uncertainty that we talked about at the start of this chapter. And yes, this is another big clue!

Let's look at these deeper questions more closely. For starters, try asking them of yourself. Take each question seriously, and take your time fishing for answers. Ask yourself each question in turn. What's my life about? Who am I?

We're willing to bet that these questions are very difficult for you. So difficult in fact that a common reaction is for people to think, 'This is awful! I'm ashamed to admit that I don't know. Surely others must know. Why don't I?' What follows is often self-doubt and a feeling of unworthiness in not having the answers to such basic questions. Once you realise that this is perfectly normal, that most others are in the same boat, you can have a little chuckle, forgive yourself, and begin with a fresh and open curiosity to learn about yourself.

Let's explore then. There's an old Chinese proverb that says,

What do you really want to accomplish?

'Where you're coming from is where you're going to.' For example, if you're coming from 'serving', then you're going to go where your serving takes you. This will be a different destination for your life than if you were coming from 'anger'. If you want to understand what your life's about, which is one of our deeper questions, then look at where you're coming from.

Where are you coming from? No doubt we've all had the experience of seeing someone's behaviour and trying to figure out where they're coming from. We do this because we intuitively understand that where they're coming from is driving the person's behaviour. Of course, the same is true for ourselves — where we're coming from is driving our behaviours too.

It's not as easy though, to figure out where you're coming from. That's because where you're coming from is so familiar to you that it has become 'part of the furniture'. Even so, if you focus on it, you can learn to see it. A simple but effective way of seeing it is to work backwards from your behaviours, because we know that they're driven by where you're coming from. Consider, for example, how you behave in a conversation with another person. How do you want to come across? Do you want to be right? To be friendly? To be taken seriously? To be the wounded one? Whatever you want to be, your energies are engaged in the pursuit of that wanting, whether you're conscious of that or not at the time. And the fact that you're putting energy into that pursuit says that that's where you're coming from. So, how do you want to come across? Is there one way that stands out? Is there a theme?

A key aspect to consider here is where you're coming from in relation to what you want. We noted earlier that 'want' comes from a feeling of lack, whereas love and desire lead to passion and energy to create and take risks. If you see in yourself that you're coming from a feeling of lack, then an obvious question is lack of what? Earlier, we suggested that focusing on what you really love and truly desire would bring you to your real purpose in life, and that's true. However if your lack is profound, you may need to face up to it and deal with it in order to free yourself from being driven by it. As always, it's your choice!

Beyond where you're coming from, there's a deeper layer again. That's because where you're coming from is driven by who you are. Now, it might seem daft to suggest that people don't know who they are, but in our experience, most people have only a vague idea of who they are. Amazing perhaps, but we see this all the time.

> *You can demonstrate this to yourself by asking yourself the question, 'Who am I?' over and over, demanding a fresh answer each time. Remember though, that answers like 'I'm a father' or 'I'm tall' are what you are, not who you are. This makes it pretty tough to answer. Just keep asking the question, and see what your mind supplies in the way of answers. Then imagine that all of your answers are like puzzle pieces on the surface of a sphere, and that 'you' are at the centre. By building up a mosaic of answers that define the surface, you can begin to get a good sense of who is at the centre. Get the idea? Why not try it now. Who am I?*

If you find yourself flagging in this search, remember that knowing what you want is based on knowing who you are. So, if you've got only a vague idea of what you want in life, it's probably because you've got only a vague idea of who you are. Persevere! You need to know!

We do acknowledge that the self-discovery process can be quite painful. As human beings we are imperfect, so knowing ourselves means facing up to these imperfections. We tend to avoid, perhaps strongly, exploring ourselves too deeply. Do you feel that aversion now, just from thinking about it? There's no doubt in our minds that this avoidance is a key limit to people understanding themselves well enough to truly see their own lives clearly and so understand their real purpose.

The good news is that once you wake up to who you really are, you can then start to create who you want to become, and that's what this book is all about.

A key characteristic that strongly defines who you are is your unique set of personal differences from other people. What is it that makes you you, and not someone else?

Another key characteristic that strongly defines who you are is your unique set of personal limitations. What are your personal limits? If we could list all of these things, we could use that list to 'pigeon-hole' you in a box. 'Your' box would then represent who you are by defining what's unique about you and what your unique limits are.

We all have our box. The key point is that we all have limits. None of us is infinite! As we grow and develop through life those limits change. Some of them expand, whereas others close in. The space inside our box thus represents our comfort zone, while the space outside our box, which is infinite, represents our learning zone. When we learn something, we push our limits outwards, our box expands, and thus we grow as a person.

Who's in Charge of Your Life?

By definition, what you truly desire is outside your current box, otherwise you already have it! To accomplish what you truly desire, you need to expand your box. You can do this the hard way, by pushing energetically at your limits, but when you engage yourself in pushing at your limits, your focus is on your limits, whereas your focus really needs to be on your learning. There's a saying which goes, 'What you resist will persist, because where your focus goes, your energy flows.' This is another very big clue!

Rather than pushing at your limits, a better way is to 'occupy' some of the space outside your box. We call this 'getting out of your box'. When you do this, by definition your box expands to include the new space. Makes sense?

The question is, how do you do that? To answer that you need to understand the limits the walls of your box represent are self-imposed. They define your comfort zone. Granted, they have mostly been constructed by your parents, teachers and others when you were young, but it's you who is now keeping them in place by allowing yourself to be limited by them. The reason you need to get out of your box is that there are no truly new possibilities in your box, which is built from your already existing history and experience. However, outside the comfort zone, there is your learning zone and its size is infinite!

Getting out of your box is much more significant than it might seem. There is evidence from some insightful work by Harvard professor Abraham Zaleznik (and others) that really exceptional leaders have often gone through a personal crisis in their adult lives. Their crisis was powerful enough to break down the walls of their existing box and force them to reassess it from the ground up. The point is that as a result of their crisis they have rebuilt their box themselves, as adults, so they now know it in a way that they never consciously did before, when it was largely built by others.

Armed with this knowledge these people now know themselves, they know what's really important, and they know that if they really need to they can rebuild their box yet again. They have power over their own destiny and potentially the destiny of others.

Their rebuilt boxes are also expanded, because they now contain all they did before and more. In this way, these people have grown.

Halfway through I had a sudden realisation that I could achieve or be anything I wanted to be. The capability was always there, but it was dormant. — M.

A big question then, is: can this be done without a personal crisis? It's clear that precious things lost can get you out of your box. We propose that what you truly desire can also get you out of your box. Arguably it's harder to jump out than be pushed out, so to speak, but that's where your desire comes in. If you desire something enough, you will jump out of your box to get it, ignoring your current limits.

Actually, you already intuitively know how to do this. In fact, when you were a child you did it all the time. You stood up. You wrote. You talked. You rode a bike. All because you truly desired to do so. You simply decided to do it. You ignored your limits and you just did it. Recapture that ability now and step outside your box again to accomplish what you truly desire in your life.

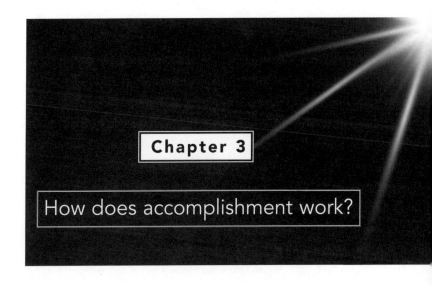

Chapter 3

How does accomplishment work?

Once you're clear about what you truly desire to accomplish in your lifetime, the next obvious step is to go forth and accomplish it! This is where the fun starts!

Naturally, there are many factors to consider and integrate in order to accomplish something. Things like establishing a workable game plan, gathering and applying the needed resources, and perhaps getting the support of others. You may also need money, premises, equipment, tools, or a host of other things. Even when you're completely clear about what you want to accomplish, these 'operational' factors will have to be successfully addressed before it will actually be accomplished.

No doubt there's much knowledge and there are many texts on how to master each of these factors. What we've seen though, is that there are some less-than-obvious underlying principles that powerfully influence accomplishment. These principles are about how you as a person approach the tasks that lead to accomplishment. We describe these simply as the 'Principles of Accomplishment'. In this chapter, we'll consider eight key principles, looking at each in turn for the learning it brings.

The first and most important principle is <u>Decide</u>.
You need to decide specifically, clearly and positively what you're going to accomplish.

> *I came away knowing I had to change my life, and I did. I wrote down three things I'd do, and I went and did them. — M.*

This principle is so critical that we devoted the previous chapter to exploring it in detail. There is, however, a further point we'd like to make here. We've noticed that people sometimes hold back from deciding because they're concerned that once they take such a momentous decision, they'll be stuck with it for life. People intuitively know that things change as time passes, so for some people a 'whole of life' decision taken now looms as a possible straitjacket later.

The key issue here is that it's you who's taking the decision, so you can choose to apply navigation or course correction to your decision as time passes. You're in charge. Thus you can ensure that your decision stands for as long as it makes sense, but you're always free to change it if and when you need to.

> *Learning this principle gave me the focus I needed. It strengthened my ability to take charge and be in control. I discovered that the decision was mine — I could take charge and make a difference. — D.*

The second principle is <u>Be Committed</u>.

When you're on a diving board, you're not committed until you've jumped. Of course you don't jump recklessly. You look carefully before you leap. And you jump just as carefully, because you know that you can hurt yourself badly if you hit the water the wrong way. But, having taken all that into account, you do jump, even knowing there's no going back, no changing your mind halfway down. That's commitment.

The diving metaphor makes commitment very clear, but in other walks of life it's not always that clear, and it's sometimes easy to lose sight of completely. For example, if you undertake to do something for someone, do you give the undertaking as carefully and see it through with the same follow-through as if you'd jumped off a diving board?

In accomplishing the outcomes you want in your life, commitment means keeping your focus on creating the results you truly desire. Make no mistake, the result will occur 90–99 percent of the time because of your intention and commitment and only 1–10 percent because of your action and technique. The bottom line is: no commitment, no result. If you're truly committed you won't be deflected from accomplishing the outcomes you want. Even if you get off the path somehow, if you know your destination before you set off, you'll always be able to re-find the path, or even make a new one.

The third principle is <u>Be Honest</u>.

Face your results or your lack of results. Be honest with yourself, and be honest with others. A simple and effective test is to look directly at your eyes in a mirror. Are you truly honest with yourself? Really? About everything? If not, why not? Who do you think you're fooling? And more importantly, why are you doing it?

> *My honesty with myself was weak — I used to say what others wanted to hear. — M.*

Our view is that people who are being dishonest with themselves are doing so because the truths they'd have to face if they did are truths they'd rather not face. This little story from De Mello[2] called 'The Truth Shop' says it all:

> *I could hardly believe my eyes when I saw the name of the shop: The Truth Shop. The saleswoman was very polite: 'What type of truth do you wish to purchase, partial or whole?' The whole truth of course. No deceptions for me, no defences, no rationalisations. I wanted my truth plain and unadulterated.*
>
> *She waved me on to another side of the store. The salesman there pointed to the price tag. 'The price is very high, sir,' he said. 'What is it?' I asked, determined to get the whole truth, no matter what it cost. 'Your security, sir,' he answered. I came away with a heavy heart. I still need the safety of my unquestioned beliefs.*

We acknowledge that facing up to your own truths can be painful, but as you probably already know, not facing up to your truths strongly inhibits you from accomplishing what you truly desire. It's also hard to know yourself if you're not honest with yourself, with all the consequences that we have discussed in the last chapter. Once again, it's your choice: face your truths and grow, or avoid your truths and be stuck.

How does accomplishment work?

On the other side of the coin, the benefits of facing up to your own truths are considerable. You'll be able to respect yourself for your courage, which in turn allows others to see your courage and to respect you for it, which in turn makes it possible for them to follow your lead, which ultimately helps you to accomplish the outcomes you want. You'll also know that you're not a cheat, which will allow you to genuinely put yourself on the line when it's needed, which could make the crucial go/no-go difference at any given point.

And are you honest with others? If you need the help of others to accomplish what you truly desire, and let's face it you probably do, then honesty is not just the best policy, it's the only policy. The fact is, people can usually tell if you're dishonest in even little ways, and the damage that does to your credibility, and therefore to their willingness to help you, is immense. How willing would you be to give your precious energy to someone's cause when you saw that they weren't being honest with you? And how easy would it be for you to tell if someone was being less than honest with you?

I say honesty comes first. It frustrates the hell out of me that people don't do that. If people were more honest from the outset, it'd be so much easier. — M.

It's more challenging than it seems. For example, do you always live up to your word? If you say to someone, 'I'll get back to you tomorrow', do you always do so? Or did you ever tell your child you'd be at their school sports and then not show up? Every missed commitment counts. You notice when other people miss their commitments, and they notice when you do.

You can deal with anything if you've got honesty, because from honesty comes trust and with trust you can communicate.
— T.

The fourth principle is <u>Express Yourself</u>.

Communicate what is real for you, including your emotions. Sadly, we've learnt to hide our emotions all too well, especially in the business world. We're taught in business not to get emotional about things — to be cool, calm and collected at all times. Even in our personal lives we're taught to conceal emotions — 'Big boys don't cry', or 'Don't let him see that he's upset you.' We intuitively know that this is false, but the social pressure to conform is strong, especially when we're growing up.

The problem with this approach is that inscrutability has its price tag, and it's very high. A classic example of this is the effect that sunglasses have. It's well known that if people wear sunglasses then you can't make eye contact with them, so you don't connect with them, and you can't trust them. What's less well known is that the same is true if people mask the way they express their thoughts or feelings. We intuitively know that we're seeing a mask. That makes us wary and blocks trust. Think of someone you know who masks themselves like that. Do you feel wary of them? Do you trust them? Do you wonder what they're masking? Do you assume that what they're masking is less than wholesome? The point is that a key part of honesty is *emotional* honesty, and that means expressing yourself and what's real for you.

How does accomplishment work?

After an interview they came back to me and said, 'You're very measured, very controlled, but where's the real you?' I discovered that people want to see who you really are and what you have to offer. They don't want the façade, the corporate gloss. I'm a lot more me now — I'm prepared to let people in, let them see me. — T.

Now this doesn't mean bleed all over people emotionally! What it means is to communicate what's real for you, not some cover-up. This takes practice, patience with yourself, and courage, because your social conditioning in this area is likely to be quite strong. It's part of your 'box', as we discussed in the last chapter. The good news is that if you persevere you'll eventually realise that the masks you put on take quite a bit of energy to maintain, and as you learn to release them you feel more free, more honest, more real to others and more true to yourself.

From this principle I learnt to turn away the barriers that we create for ourselves out of a lack of self-belief, to let people see the real me, and be comfortable with vulnerability. Sharing myself with people has allowed me to achieve far more than before. — B.

The bottom line is that when people perceive you as honest they're more willing to become enrolled in helping you to accomplish the outcomes you want, and that's critical to your success in achieving what you truly desire. And there's no faking it — only genuine honesty will do!

The fifth principle is <u>Risk Yourself</u>.

We're not talking about gambling here; we're talking about breaking through your limitations. Risk and exposure are things most people fear, having 'learnt' that the price can be painful — *can be*.

The trouble is that avoiding risk so you can avoid the *possibility* of painful consequences is in the end self-defeating. *Of course*, revealing your thoughts and feelings involves taking risks. And moving past your current limitations, in other words out of your box, also involves taking risks. You're risking failure, or ridicule, condemnation, strong emotions in return, aggression, or a host of other expected and unexpected responses.

But there's also learning, and there's also a host of positive responses. You're open to growth, praise, support, connection, enrolment, love, and a meeting of minds and hearts. We're very clear that the positive results of taking risks by being open are *essential ingredients* in accomplishing what you truly desire. The thing is, people almost certainly need the support and enrolment of others to accomplish what they truly desire. Isn't that true for you?

At the risk of stating the obvious, since the positive results of risk are only available to you if you actually engage in risk, if you risk nothing, you'll accomplish nothing. That's what the old saying 'Nothing ventured, nothing gained' is about. So, take a risk; by doing so you'll unlock a critical door on the path to accomplishing what you truly desire.

How does accomplishment work?

This principle taught me to take risks. Without that learning, as a career banker of 25 years, which is all about covering your risks, I doubt if I'd have taken the risks that I did in going out and doing what I truly wanted. It changed my life. — M.

This is a good test of your true desire. If you just want something, chances are that you won't be willing to break through your limitations or risk yourself very far for it. But if you truly desire it, then you're not likely to be put off the path to accomplishing it just because you need to risk yourself along the way. So how's what you truly desire looking now? Does it pass this test? Do you?

The sixth principle is <u>Participate 100 Percent</u>.

You need to participate to get results. You can't catch fish by watching them. You need to become involved. In fact, the more involved you become, the better your fishing will be. As the best anglers know, you catch fish best when you're *totally involved*. You're knowledgeable, you're equipped, you're prepared, you're positioned, you're keen, you're skilled, you're focused, you're relaxed, and you're *loving it!*

Does this sound like you? In your drive to accomplish what you truly desire, are you participating 100 percent? Or does 100 percent participation seem a little extreme and unnecessary to you? Interestingly, it's actually *much easier* to participate 100 percent than say 90 percent. To take a simple example, it's much harder to fish successfully without the right attitude, but how many of us do that anyway, because we're only participating 90 percent? If you participate only 90 percent in accomplishing what you truly desire, in our experience there's a good

chance that you'll end up not accomplishing it. We see 90 percent participation as a big signal that all's not well.

If this sounds like you then it's time to have a good hard look
at yourself and what you're going to accomplish. How serious
are you about it after all? Are you perhaps doing it because you
feel you ought to, or even that you have to, or are you doing it
based on what you truly desire? Our advice is if you're doing it
for any other reason than your own true desire, then it's back to
square one. Tough? Yes. But if you don't face up to yourself at
this point, when will you? And if you're not real with yourself,
how will you accomplish the outcomes you want in your life?

The seventh principle is <u>Take Responsibility</u>.

Very topical, considering what we've just been talking about!
We propose that you alone are responsible for your actions and
for the results you achieve. The essence of this principle is, 'If
it's to be, it's up to me.' Do you accept that for yourself?

> *I discovered that whatever I portrayed into the environment
> was what I got back. I concluded that life's as good as you make
> it. — M.*

In the world of business it's very common to find people who
are responsible for achieving a result that's only partly within
their direct influence. It's also very common to find such people arguing that they didn't achieve the required results because
of 'influences beyond their control'. Behind this argument is
what appears to be the quite sound logic that a person cannot
be held responsible for things they don't control. This logic is
technically correct, and it's also the slippery slope to failure!

How so? Well, valid though a reason for failure might be, it's still a failure. If you readily accept lack of control over external influences as a valid reason for failure, then most of the time you will fail, because most of the time there are opposing external influences in play. If you treat the accomplishment of the outcomes you want in your life this way, then stand by to fail!

The answer? We're willing to bet that if their lives were at stake, the 'victims' of external influences would suddenly come up with a dazzling array of ways to succeed *despite* the external influences. They'd block, thrust, parry, twist, turn, wheedle, cajole, bluster, bypass, reinforce, adapt, argue, do without, humour, redouble — to a fertile mind the list is pretty well endless. And why? Because they *truly desire* to accomplish something. That's the power of true desire. It will not be denied.

Have you noticed how children often end up accomplishing what they truly desire, despite the obvious fact that they don't have direct control over many (if any) of the relevant influences? How do they do that? How did you do that when you were a kid? Sure, many of their methods are immature and perhaps some are less than honourable. But the *key* is that they take *full responsibility* on *themselves* for getting what they want. Kids can do that. You did when you were a kid, and you still can if you really want to, and in our experience you'll need to. So if this attitude has escaped you as you grew up, then reclaim it!

The eighth and final principle is <u>Work in Partnership</u>.
The essence of this principle is, 'If it's to be, it's up to *we*.' When working with other people, work for mutual benefit. This doesn't just mean 'support the principle' of mutual benefit; it means *work* for it.

Work just as hard to ensure that the other person wins as you do to ensure that you win.

To some this will seem to be a new burden — here you are 100 percent involved in accomplishing what you truly desire and now we're proposing that you work just as hard for others to ensure that they win too. And if there are many others won't that mean many times the work?

Actually, no. These people are putting their energy into your project because doing so adds value to their lives in some way, and that's how they get their success from contributing. That means you're not required to put a similar amount of energy into their projects, but you *do* need to work hard to ensure that your support people get their success, whatever that might be for them.

It also means that you need to understand their real reasons for being involved, that you don't just 'take' their effort and say 'thank you very much'. You need to connect with them at a personal level, and become their partner in such a way that you're both ensuring that you both succeed. They're giving you success; consider it your responsibility to give them their success.

Of course the 'win-win' theme is very well known. What we've noticed is that while people understand and readily agree with the concept, more often than not they don't truly deliver on it. How about you? If you're really honest with yourself, do you truly deliver on it?

I'd always felt that I was a win-win person, but a learning game we played revealed my kill-kill tendencies, which I would've absolutely denied if asked. — J.

How does accomplishment work?

At the end of the day people are often still most interested in getting help for what they want, whereas they really need to be enlisting partners who they can work together with to achieve their mutual goals.

> *I was a stressed-out workaholic. It wasn't good for me and didn't make me a good leader. Through these principles I learnt to trust others. It was a breakthrough on a big personal issue for me. I now have an enormous sense of respect for the individual. I don't think I'd have survived in my job the way I was. — T.*

These are the eight Principles of Accomplishment. As you will have seen they're not at all about the mechanics of accomplishment. They're about you and how you approach the task you propose to accomplish. We know from our experience and from seeing how successful people approach their tasks that if you use these principles fully and energetically, you'll be well on the way to accomplishing what you truly desire in your life.

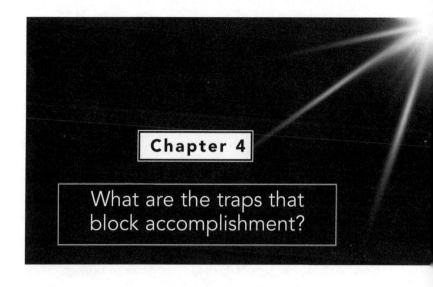

Chapter 4

What are the traps that block accomplishment?

Few would argue that accomplishing a worthwhile outcome takes, amongst other things, considerable energy. It's like rolling a ball towards a particular spot. If you leave it alone for a while it rolls to a stop. If the way forward is sloping up or sideways, it takes more energy and more frequent attention to keep it going and to keep it on the right path. Even if the way forward is downhill, it takes more energy to stop it from rolling away and perhaps missing the target altogether. Often there are obstacles too, things that need to be jumped over, pushed through, tackled head on, or just plain avoided.

In a similar way, moving along the path to accomplishment takes energy and attention, and it contains obstacles. We've already talked about how to effectively focus your energy and attention to accomplish the outcomes that you truly desire. In this chapter we'll look at dealing with obstacles.

There are no doubt many texts on how to deal with obstacles to accomplishment. However, in our experience, the most telling obstacles are those which rise up from within us, the ones we erect ourselves, ones that we don't even recognise as obstacles. 'But wait', you say, 'why on earth would we erect our own obstacles?' Well, we wouldn't, not deliberately, but once again the way we *approach* accomplishment contains a range of conscious and subconscious behaviours, some of which are very helpful, and some of which are very unhelpful. It's our unhelpful behaviours that are our obstacles.

We've identified thirteen specific behaviours that are significant obstacles to accomplishment. We call these 'Mind Traps', and we'll look at each of them in turn. As we go through them, be watchful for evidence of them in yourself. Ask yourself: 'Is this me? Do I do that?'

The first five mind traps deal with the way we handle *ourselves* on the journey to accomplishment. They describe how we prepare our excuses in advance, in case we don't make the headway we'd intended to when we first set off.

The first mind trap is <u>Tryer</u>.

How many times have you said, 'Well, I'll try', or even 'I'll try my best.' Probably quite a few times. But what's wrong with that? After all, it wouldn't do to promise something unless we're certain we're going to deliver, so if we're genuinely unsure, isn't it more truthful to say 'I'll try'?

The point is, often the situation or the people involved need you to make a commitment. If you know that, then nothing short of giving that commitment and living up to it will do. Trouble is, you also know that giving a commitment and then missing it is 'bad'. So if you've got any doubt about definitely delivering, it seems like a good self-protective move to hedge your commitment, just in case you 'can't' deliver. And the best and easiest way to do that is to say 'I'll try.' Then if you don't deliver, well hey, you only promised to try, didn't you?

There are several problems with this scenario. The first is that you know that saying you'll 'try' gives you the leeway not to deliver, so when pressed you can and probably will over-promise. It's like overbooking a plane — it will fly with all seats full but some people who have paid for a ticket and need to fly won't be on it. Similarly, over-promising means that you're guaranteeing in advance that some of what you've promised to 'try' to deliver simply won't happen. So you're setting yourself up for some inevitable non-delivery.

This mind trap is particularly common in people who find it hard to say 'no' to other people. Interestingly, if you research how those other people feel about that, you find that they'd *much rather* be told 'Sorry, no' than be told 'I'll try.' Why? Because if they're not going to get it anyway they'd rather know now and thus have time to find another way.

The second thing is that there are things that you really do need to deliver, and having let yourself off by saying you'll 'try' means that you're less likely to deliver now because you feel you've not really committed to do so. But in the eyes of the person who needs you to deliver this thing, all that matters is that you *do deliver*, and not doing so is a failure on your part, regardless of why. Therefore by saying 'I'll try', you're making a significant failure more likely to happen.

This, therefore, is a mind trap to strongly avoid. How? By either committing, or saying no, right from the start. Remember that commitment is one of the key principles of accomplishment, and that being honest with yourself and others by saying 'no' when that's needed is another principle of accomplishment. Learn to catch yourself saying the word 'try', and get out of the damaging habit of saying it. Make a start by committing to yourself now to do that.

The second mind trap is <u>Worry/Hope</u>.

The whole essence of worry is that it's about negative issues. You worry about problems and potential problems like constraints or setbacks. The trouble is, 'Where your focus goes, your energy flows.' Thus the energy you expend worrying is lost from positive issues like harnessing support.

Of course, when there aren't many constraints and setbacks facing you this may not seem like such a big deal. However, problems don't come in at a steady pace, and when they're coming thick and fast you can spend so much time worrying about them that you completely lose your ability to make progress.

As a first step to avoid this mind trap you can be aware of worrying and just say 'stop'. Then you can focus on the positive side of how you'll accomplish the outcomes you want. The benefits can be enormous. In effect you're empowering yourself to reach past the problems, rather than battling through them.

We acknowledge that for many people this is easier said than done. If this is so for you, then we suggest the following simple method for reaching past your problems.

> *Imagine that you're in the future, say a few months, and at that time the reality is that you* have solved *a particular problem. From that vantage point, the reality is that you were successful in moving past that problem. Imagine then that someone asks you, 'How did you solve*

> *that problem a few months back?' Think back on how you did it, and in the process describe an entirely plausible method by which you solved that problem. Then come back into the present and go and apply that method to your problem. You can also use this approach in a group or team setting to move past difficult problems. In our experience, this approach is far more productive than endlessly worrying about your problems.*

'Hope' is similar, except that it can be both positive and negative. You might hope for good things, or hope for problems not to occur. The negative version of 'hope' is a close cousin of 'worry', so we suggest that you give it the same treatment as 'worry'. The positive version of 'hope' seems at first glance to be useful, but on closer inspection it's a cousin of 'tryer'. By hoping that something positive will happen, you're side-stepping your own responsibility to 'deliver' it. We therefore suggest that you give it the same treatment as 'tryer'.

The third mind trap is <u>Doubt</u>.

Doubting yourself or doubting others, or both: simply put, doubt paralyses action. It sets up a dynamic of fear and procrastination that freezes you and stops forward movement.

> *Self-doubt was my biggest mind trap. It came down to the word 'I' — I always felt that I had to explain and justify using the word 'I' — it felt so introverted, egocentric, win-lose. But I came to see that my ability to achieve my vision depended on my own self-confidence. — B.*

In effect, doubt is the opposite of 'decide', the first and most critical Principle of Accomplishment. Doubt is therefore a very damaging mind trap. We suggest that you approach doubt by focusing instead on 'decide'. So if you have a real issue with doubt, then we suggest that you revisit the section on 'decide' in the last chapter.

The fourth mind trap is <u>Confusion</u>.

This is very similar in its effect to 'doubt'. If you're confused about something, you'll find it very hard to reach a decision. This whole area of doubt/confusion/uncertainty is nothing short of a heaven-sent opportunity to avoid making a decision, if that's what you want. In our experience, this 'decision avoidance' lies at the heart of doubt/confusion/uncertainty.

The question is, why do we avoid decisions that could block our accomplishment? While we might passionately want to accomplish the outcomes we want overall, there may well be things we need to do along the way that are outside our current comfort zone. In our experience, a primary reason for decision avoidance is that we already know that the answer will require us to operate outside our comfort zone.

Once you recognise that this is the underlying 'game' that's driving your doubt/confusion/uncertainty, you can address the issue more directly. You can acknowledge the real issue, and then make a conscious decision about moving outside your comfort zone and into your zone of learning. In our experience, most people want to grow, and this is where the rubber meets the road on the personal growth issue. Go for it! If you truly desire to grow, this is your big opportunity!

The fifth mind trap is <u>Regret</u>.

While not so obvious as some of the other mind traps, this one is part of a particularly vicious downward spiral.

Regret is rooted in 'should have' and 'if only'. A twinge of regret may be natural after a mistake or a failure — it's part of the learning process — but lasting regret means that you're beating yourself up for your mistake, or even for someone else's. Not surprisingly this erodes your self-confidence, in turn making you less able to confidently take decisions going forward and leading to a degree of self-paralysis. All of this can greatly impact your progress towards accomplishing the outcomes you want.

To make matters worse your personal response to your mistake or failure may well include shame, guilt, or feelings of worthlessness, all of which are very self-destructive and greatly damage your ability to accomplish the outcomes you want.

Our advice? What's past is done. You can regret it or you can learn from it. It's your choice. Take responsibility for the fact that you're beating yourself up, and consciously move on from that behaviour to a learning stance.

I learnt never to look back. If one door closes, there's another waiting to be opened. — *D.*

The next three mind traps deal with the way we handle *others* on the journey to accomplishment. They describe how we behave inappropriately in our efforts to secure the help of others, in the process perhaps damaging our chances of successfully accomplishing the outcomes we want.

This group starts with the sixth mind trap, Explanation.

This mind trap is most commonly found in management. At first glance it isn't obvious that 'explanation' is a mind trap, but it is.

There's a fairly standard management ritual that demands an explanation when an expected result is not achieved. What's needed is a brief and factual explanation; we don't see this as a mind trap but a natural part of the *management process.*

However, because an explanation is a statement of the reasons for non-delivery of results, it is at its heart defensive. Because of this our explanations are often much more about our reasons and stories for why we didn't do or won't be doing what was needed. Are your alarm bells ringing yet? If not, have another look at the seventh Principle of Accomplishment in the last chapter, and you'll see how 'explanation' opposes 'taking responsibility'. You'll also see our suggestions on ways to eliminate this damaging mind trap.

The seventh mind trap is Self-righteousness.

Many volumes have been written about the human ego and egocentric behaviour. This behaviour results in people giving their own point of view more credence than the viewpoints that others express. This is not necessarily a 'bad' thing! Problems arise when the essential balance between our viewpoint and that of others isn't maintained. We become 'captured' by the 'rightness' of our own viewpoint, giving it more weight than is healthy for our relationships with those around us. People who are very knowledgeable are particularly at risk of self-righteous behaviour.

What are the traps that block accomplishment?

Self-righteousness is about our unwillingness or inability to accommodate anyone else's viewpoint. It's fairly obvious that this damages our relationship with the people who hold those other viewpoints, and this in turn damages our ability to secure and maintain their support for our goals. The saying that 'people hate a know-it-all' is a big clue! Self-righteousness is therefore self-defeating. A more useful approach would be to recognise that there are many viewpoints that need to be accommodated in a positive way.

The sad reality is that many people have trapped themselves in their need to be right. If you're one of them, ask yourself this: would you rather be right or be friends? The point is that realistically you can't be both. We're willing to bet that very few people would rather be right than be friends. So if you're busy being right all the time, then it's time to realise that the damage this is doing to your relationships isn't worth it, and that it's time for a personal shake-up. It's also time to realise that any damage to your relationships is damage to your accomplishment.

I used to be pretty bullet-proof, but now I see that in this world you'll never achieve anything in isolation — you need other people to make it work. — D.

We suggest that a useful way to eliminate this damaging mind trap is to acknowledge that the very people you 'know better than' are probably 'better than you' at relationships, and are therefore 'better than you' at accomplishing the outcomes they want. This helps you respect their overall 'different but equal' status with you, which makes it less likely that you'll feel 'superior' to them and thus behave in a self-righteous way in the future.

We've seen some impressive results when people effectively move themselves out of the self-righteousness mind trap. Their relationships flourish, they have a glow of inner happiness at being truly connected with others, perhaps for the first time in a long time, and they accelerate seemingly effortlessly towards accomplishing the outcomes they want.

> *I'd been an individual expert before — now my style is to get it done through other people. That's enabled me to achieve far more than before. — B.*

The eighth mind trap is <u>Con Man or Con Woman</u>.

How tempting it can be, when you really need something from someone but know you won't get it if you're honest with them, to use a little deceit and, hey presto! you've got what you want.

Let's face it, who among us is such a saint that they've never done that and never will? No doubt many of us have exaggerated or manipulated information to get what we want at some time or other. Have you?

You already know this, but let's say it anyway: the problem is that people often find out that they've been conned, and *next time* you need something from them you're in big trouble. So honesty is not just the best way, it's the *only* way.

Interestingly, sometimes people's love for others or their own self-interest can result in them being willing to be conned more than once. This makes it especially attractive for the con man or woman to continue conning them. However, this leads to an ever-increasing 'debt', which ultimately results in loss of respect and/or a king-sized piece of trouble when enough is finally enough. Either way, you can see how comprehensively this mind trap destroys your ability to secure people's longer-term help in accomplishing the outcomes you want.

The last five mind traps deal with the way we handle *external obstacles* on the journey to accomplishment. They describe how we avoid accountability for setbacks or failures by laying blame outside ourselves.

This group starts with the ninth mind trap, Resentment.

If I blame you for a setback or failure, then it's your fault, not mine, and yet I'm the one who's suffered. I might resent that. In this way, resentment follows and is rooted in blame.

The *only* value in holding others to blame for setbacks or failures in the accomplishment of the outcomes you want is that it lets you take yourself off the hook. This is why we do it! But let's face it, blaming others contributes nothing to moving you closer to accomplishing the outcomes you want. In fact it's counter-productive. You could be making headway if you accepted accountability and got on with it, but instead you're making no headway because you're too busy blaming someone else and resenting them for it. You might even be seeking revenge!

If this mind trap is one you recognise in yourself, we recommend that you revisit the seventh principle of accomplishment. You'll see how 'blame' and 'resentment' oppose 'taking responsibility'. You'll also see our suggestions on ways to eliminate this mind trap.

I resented that my father was inattentive to me as a child. Seeing that this was a mind trap helped me face up to it. I went away and challenged my father about it, and we successfully worked through it. — M.

The tenth mind trap is <u>Resignation</u>.

The theme here is, 'There's nothing I can do about it. What's the use? I give up.' Hopelessness and despair reign.

What this mind trap does is put responsibility for failure on to an external force too strong to oppose. Once again it's an avoidance of personal responsibility for getting the desired results and accomplishing the outcomes you want. And once again, the seventh Principle of Accomplishment, 'take responsibility', is an antidote we recommend.

No doubt there are external forces too powerful to overcome, but there's also no doubt that people who give up mostly do so in the face of forces that they could overcome if they really set their mind to it. The saying 'when the going gets tough, the tough get going' is a reminder to us all of the power of true commitment. So if you're caught in this mind trap, we also recommend that you review the second Principle of Accomplishment, 'commitment'.

The eleventh mind trap is <u>Cynicism</u>.

Is there perhaps some cynic in us all? You might be surprised at just how comprehensively self-defeating cynicism really is.

Have you ever been faced with a through-and-through cynic? How did you relate to them inside yourself? A typical reaction to cynics is, 'If it's as bad as you're playing it, then why are you still here?' In other words, people see cynicism as basically dishonest.

What are the chances that you would follow a cynic, that you'd be willing to respect them as your leader? We bet your answer is 'not much chance'. And conversely, how many outstanding leaders do you notice being cynical? We bet your answer is 'none I can think of'.

If you're a cynic you're more or less completely torpedoing any possibility that people will give their energy to helping you accomplish the outcomes you want.

Just as importantly, cynicism also comes from blaming others for 'the situation', for which reason the observations we've made about the 'resentment' mind trap also apply to the cynicism mind trap. Interestingly, once cynics wake up to the enormous harm they are doing to themselves, they often miraculously let their 'cloak' of cynicism fall away. Now that really tells you something about cynicism, doesn't it!? Our advice is that if you're a cynic, wake up and let it go.

I've seen many people go through this wake-up now. I love seeing how the cynic gets washed out of them, how their appetite for learning becomes so strong. — B.

The twelfth mind trap is <u>Disassociation</u>.

This person is apathetic. Their theme is, 'I can't accept it, but I can't change it, so now I don't care.' Whatever 'it' is, you can be sure that it was a major event for the disassociated person. Why else would it cause such a powerful emotional reaction?

The key to disassociation lies in the 'I can't' part of the rationale. The fact is, you can if you choose to. One option is to just accept 'it', however unpalatable that might be. At least that way you're able to move on, regroup, rebuild, and reconnect with the outcomes you want and set about accomplishing them. The alternative is to remain stuck, disassociated, with your feelings suppressed. So you're going to be much better off by accepting it, wouldn't you say?

Another possibility is that maybe you can change 'it'. As always, it's really your choice. One thing is sure though — if you choose to sink into disassociation it's 'game over' as far as accomplishing the outcomes you want is concerned.

The thirteenth and last mind trap is <u>Victim</u>.

In our view the victim theme runs through a number of other mind traps, so we're going to give it major attention. Look back over the last six mind traps and you'll see how the transfer of blame on to an external party is founded in victim-hood. The theme is 'I'm not to blame — they are.'

We all understand what it is to be a victim. It means that someone 'did it to us'. We were wronged, damaged, hurt, and it wasn't our fault at all, it was all the doing of the offender. We see daily evidence of real crimes, real perpetrators and real victims. Our society accepts the concept of victim-hood and provides extensive and much-needed formal and informal victim support.

This is a natural and vital part of a caring society. Every day there are instances where people become real victims of the misdeeds of others. For people in these circumstances, victim-hood is not a mind trap, and the spontaneous and generous support of others can be vital to restoring their well-being.

So what's the problem? Are there circumstances in which victim-hood can be a mind trap? The short answer is yes. Most of us feel the need for sympathy from time to time, and in itself even that is not a mind trap. When it becomes a mind trap is when you 'use' people's caring response to real victims as a way to 'get' sympathy when you're not a real victim.

It's also a mind trap when someone who was once a real victim 'trades on' their victim-hood long afterwards. The point is that even if you've been a real victim you don't have to live the rest of your life like that. You didn't have a choice about what happened, but you do have a choice about what will happen next, and how you'll feel and behave. Your real victim-hood is in the past. Now *you* are responsible for how you go forward.

Victim is an easy mind trap to fall into, because it's so instinctive, and people's goodwill and support is so quickly and generously extended to real victims. But in the end, 'playing at' or 'trading on' being a victim is basically a con, and our comments about the 'con man or con woman' mind trap are also relevant here.

Unfortunately, we often manage to con ourselves in the process of conning others. Any time we're feeling hard done by we start feeling like the victim of an external perpetrator, and we start needing and looking for the solace and support of others. But if you challenge a person who is playing at being a victim about what they're doing, the typical response is firm to strong denial. 'Who me? No way!', or even anger: 'Who are you calling a victim?'

I encounter the victim mind trap the most. Now I challenge people who're being victims, but I don't use the word victim, because they would not accept seeing themselves as a victim.
— B.

Who's in Charge of Your Life?

Why do we con ourselves like that? The basic reason is that it shifts the 'blame' for whatever has gone wrong or just isn't going the way we want it, on to an external party so that we don't have to admit to ourselves that we're either partly or fully accountable. At its heart the victim mind trap is coming from blaming others to avoid facing our own accountability.

How do you feel about the proposition that you might be one that plays at or trades on being a victim? Do you feel yourself quickly dismissing that notion? Ultimately only you know if you're a real victim or not, so it's up to you to be honest with yourself and others, however tough that may be, which is one of the Principles of Accomplishment.

> *I find that victim is the place most people go first. It's a great way to explain away why you're not prepared to commit. I try to get people to see that they're opting out.* — T.

If playing at being a victim is a regular behaviour for you, here's a way to lift yourself out of that mind trap.

> *Think of a situation in which you know in your heart that you were 'playing' at being a victim. Now tell that story, but tell it from the viewpoint of being accountable for what happened. Imagine you set it up and you chose the steps, without which the situation wouldn't have happened. Now acknowledge that you weren't really a victim after all. OK, it's no fun admitting, even just to yourself, that you've been playing at being a victim, but it's also tremendously empowering. Finally, you realise that you and only you are accountable for yourself and*

What are the traps that block accomplishment?

> *what you accomplish in this life, and you can stop hiding behind 'external forces' when things go wrong. Finally, you can stand and deliver.*

Perhaps the greatest role model for people caught in the victim mind trap is Nelson Mandela. If ever anyone had a perfect opportunity to be a victim it was Nelson, and he turned it down. We can all see how tall he stands as a result.

This is the raw power of overcoming your own victim-hood. It's also probably the single most important contribution that you can make to your own success.

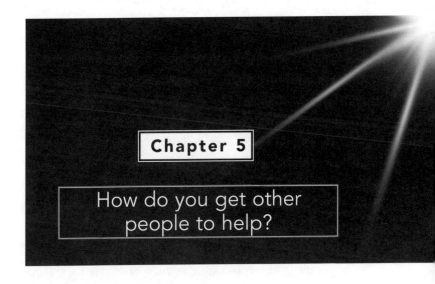

Chapter 5

How do you get other people to help?

Do you need other people to help you accomplish the outcomes you want? Not just help in the sense of people pitching in with your work, but also help in the sense of people voting for you, deciding to attend, giving you priority and a host of other things that people do to help.

Chances are, you do need people to help. This is where many a purpose has remained unaccomplished due to lack of support. You even see notices to this effect — 'event cancelled due to lack of support'!

The reality is that if you want people to help, you'll have to appeal to them for that help. You need to invite people to help, and your invitation needs to represent to them a desirable use of their time and energy which they will assess on the basis of the value that it would add to their lives to help you.

We'd like to make a special point here for managers. You are in the 'privileged' position of having formal authority over people by virtue of your position in the organisational hierarchy. It is therefore possible for you to get people to help without necessarily 'appealing' to them, using your positional power. In effect, you can 'push' them to do what you want.

Many managers do just that. It's clear that people 'go along' with this approach only to the extent that they feel they 'have to' and no more. This makes the accomplishment of an important outcome risky as it requires ongoing management attention to ensure people are continuing to contribute what's needed. Even then things often work only when people 'go the extra mile', which of course they don't if they don't have to! The 'push' approach doesn't work if people don't feel that they 'have to' comply.

All in all, getting people to help because they have to is not the best approach to accomplishing the outcomes you want. Also, outside formal hierarchies this approach is not even available! Being able to successfully appeal to people and enrol their help *because they want to* is a key capability that you'll need to develop in yourself. The acid test for managers is: if we took away your 'corporate badge', could you still stand and enrol people without it?

In our experience some people are naturally good at enrolling other people, and many more aren't. This doesn't mean that only those who are naturally good at it are going to succeed. To the contrary, there are many examples of people who have achieved great things as a result of *learning* this skill, which proves that it's not something you need to be born with.

This chapter is devoted to helping you learn the skills you need in order to get other people to help you accomplish the outcomes you want, based on them wanting to help. These are the skills of leadership. A lot has been written and said on the subject of leadership, and no doubt there will be much more in the future! Our interest is to distill this to its essence and show you how to use this effectively so that you can accomplish the outcomes you want.

Obvious as it may seem, for you to lead other people they need to follow you, so let's look at leadership by looking at what moves people to follow other people.

Basically, people will follow you if they perceive that you're going on a journey that they'd like to be on too. They need to see it as adding value to their own life, and they need to believe that you have what it takes to get them there.

Of course this is easier to say than do, but at least it's a simple concept! You can easily check and confirm that it's valid by reflecting on your own reasoning when you've followed other people. Let's look at how to get other people to volunteer their help by using this approach.

When people perceive that you're going on a journey that they'd like to be on too, they're 'drawn' to your journey. They feel a 'pull' inside themselves towards joining you. This means that if and when they do join you, they're voluntarily committing their time, energy and resources to actualising your vision. This is quite the opposite to feeling 'pushed' by you because of your position of power, and it marks out the key difference between leadership and management authority.

However, to feel this pull people must be able to 'see' your destination, and they must also 'see' a journey to that destination as being attractive to them. In other words, people need to have an appealing 'vision' in their mind about the journey and the destination. One primary skill of leadership is to implant this attractive vision in the mind of people whose help you need.

To achieve this you need to get your vision clear in your own mind first. This isn't always as easy as it sounds. You've probably had the experience where you've felt clear about something but when it came to describing it to someone else, you struggled. This usually means that it was a bit vague in your own mind to begin with. It also reveals that describing your vision is a good way to test how clear it is in your mind.

Interestingly, describing your vision is also one of the best ways to begin the process of clarifying it for yourself. As you describe your vision, you 'trip over' the bits that aren't clear yet, so you know exactly where to pinpoint further thinking and clarification. This process is called 'formulating' your vision, and it's the first step in getting people to help you to accomplish the outcomes you want.

A key point to note here is that your vision will need to be appealing to others. Ideally, so appealing that people will find it 'compelling'. To achieve this, the vision you formulate will need to bring forth in others what's in their own hearts, because that's what people find really compelling. This implies that you need the skill to sense and build on the purpose in others, which in turn implies that you need to understand what moves people and 'turns them on'. With this under-standing, you can show people the personal value for them.

The key is natural leadership — when people can make a personal connection to you they find it inspiring. After I learnt to believe in myself, people just committed to the vision and dream that I had and their collective effort made it happen. If you transfer these principles into organisations, you can achieve so much. — T.

This emphasises the importance of being immersed in the world of the people around you and understanding the purpose in them by close personal contact. Your ability to feel the purpose in others is also based on your understanding of the purpose within yourself, which again emphasises the importance of self-knowledge to effective leadership.

Begin by testing your vision on yourself. Does it call you? Does it appeal to you? Would you be willing to voluntarily commit your time, energy and resources to it? The bottom line is that if it doesn't call loudly to you, then it certainly won't call others. Will it stretch you enough to be a true vision? If it won't stretch you, then it isn't a vision, it's a goal. A vision is big and all-encompassing. Test it on others too. Does it call them? What do they find attractive or unattractive about it? Be relentless in your pursuit of a compelling vision.

If you've ever seen corporate 'vision statements', you'll know that very few of them are attractive to the point of being compelling. What this tells you is that it's relatively much easier to formulate a 'vision statement' than a 'compelling vision'. What it also tells you is that it's common for people to consider that they've 'done' their vision when they've made it into a 'statement', whether that statement is interesting to others or not. We urge you not to fall into that trap, which we regard as very damaging or even fatal to the accomplishment of the outcomes you want.

Once your vision is clear and compelling in your own mind, you're then in a position to implant it in other people's minds. To achieve this, you'll need to communicate your vision clearly and effectively to other people. This process is called 'articulating' your vision. It's the first step in 'enrolling' people into your vision, and it's the most critical of leadership skills, because it's the point where people either buy in or they don't. This is the acid test of your leadership.

Perhaps sensing the momentous nature of this step, this is where a great many would-be leaders needlessly falter. Research by Kouzes and Posner has shown that the part of leadership that makes people the most uncomfortable is trying to inspire people with a vision. Interestingly, only 10 percent of people consider themselves inspiring, which means that 90 percent of us are inhibited just by the belief that we're not inspirational! Does this sound like you?

In a nutshell, this says that most people simply lack the self-confidence for leadership. For them, articulating a vision is simply outside their comfort zone. If that's true for you, then focusing on developing your willingness and ability to stand and articulate yourself may be your single most effective move in accomplishing the outcomes you want.

In our experience, people's level of comfort and enjoyment in articulating themselves is directly related to how often they do it. We emphasise that this is definitely a learnable skill, and with practice it can be turned from a weakness into a strength.

People become visionary leaders when they 'take a stand' for a new possibility and draw people into that new possibility. They're clear about their purpose and vision, they take a

stand and by articulating their vision they attract people to it
and enrol people into it. Think about people you consider to
be visionary leaders. Do they do that? Can you? Do you?
Will you?

Please note that taking a stand is not the same thing as
taking a position. When you take a stand, you declare an
interest. There are many possible positions that might fulfil
that interest, and you're open to those possibilities. By contrast, when you take a position, you're asserting that only
that position will fulfil your interest, which is very unlikely.
Visionary leaders take stands, not positions.

Let's look now to the second part of what gets people willing to follow you on a journey: they need to believe that you
have what it takes to get them there. Let's face it, who would
set off on a journey into unfamiliar territory led by a guide
they didn't believe could deliver them safely? Would you?
No. You need to feel confident that people you're considering following can and will get you there.

A good question is, what is it that people are looking for
to convince themselves that you have the leadership capabili-
ties to get them there? In our experience it's a blend of several key factors.

The first key factor is your <u>Authenticity</u> and your <u>Personal Integrity</u>.

People need to be able to trust that the 'you' they're signing
up with is the 'real' you. They need to see this so they can be
assured that you'll still be the same person they signed on
with right through the journey. How do people assess this?
They assess your integrity by whether you 'walk the talk'.

They're looking for alignment between what you say and what you do, and in our experience people are very astute at assessing this. Are you good at assessing that in others? And what about you — are your words and actions closely aligned? If you're unsure, ask people around you to give you feedback about yourself.

People are also looking to see how strongly you 'mask' yourself. We all, to a greater or lesser degree, mask our thoughts and feelings, and this is not necessarily a 'bad' thing. After all, life could be very raw if we were constantly bombarding each other with our unmasked thoughts and feelings. However, some people, probably in response to past experiences, mask themselves more heavily than normal social considerations require.

This has the 'desirable' effect of hiding and protecting vulnerabilities, but a part of other people's trust in you comes from 'seeing' your vulnerabilities. People 'know' that you have vulnerabilities. We all do. It's part of being human. In seeing your vulnerabilities, people see a consistency between 'how they know you are' and 'how they see you present yourself'.

Revealing your vulnerabilities is therefore the ultimate display of your authentic self to others. In reverse, excessive masking of your vulnerabilities blocks trust. People are very sensitive to excessive masking. Do you distrust people who are excessively masked? Do you firmly hide your own vulnerabilities, for example, behind your 'corporate badge'? Again, if you're unsure, ask people around you how they see you.

If you're one who hides yourself excessively behind masks, your ability to accomplish the outcomes you want will be greatly enhanced if you can 'drop' your masks. This is because being authentic is much more powerful than wearing and hiding behind a mask. This is the essence of the third Principle of Accomplishment, which is to be honest with yourself and others.

> *Now I'm more willing to be open about myself, which I was reluctant to do in the past. As a consequence, I'm more effective in enrolling people to a particular vision. — J.*

Dropping your masks will require care and patience. You may need some assistance from others to identify and release your masks, and to change your self-protecting behaviours. In our experience though, it's absolutely worth the effort! In fact a common view from people who have done this is that they wish they'd done it years ago, and they thoroughly recommend it to others.

The second key factor is that you've <u>Decided</u> clearly, specifically and passionately, <u>What You Want</u>.

You need to demonstrate that you know where you're going. You also need to demonstrate that you understand how to deal with things that are important to the journey at hand. As you can see, it's no accident that deciding is the first Principle of Accomplishment!

You already intuitively know how important this is. Most of us have been in situations where we naturally 'became' leaders, simply because we knew the outcomes we wanted, and how to get them, better than anyone else did at the time. Conversely, most of us have readily followed others who were clear on their destination and seemed to know how to proceed. In a complex world each of us understands only so much, and we often follow the lead of others when we think they can proceed better than we can. Thus a key to taking the lead is having a clear destination and knowing how to get there.

The third key factor is your <u>Commitment</u>.

People can smell commitment a mile off, and will elect not to join you if they perceive that you're uncommitted. Indeed, if you are uncommitted, then in our view you don't have the standing to be asking others to join you in the first place. People need to see that you yourself are 'called' to your own purpose. Believe it or not, this will be evident to others regardless of what you say or do. If you doubt this, consider how easily you notice the commitment in others when you're considering joining them on their journeys.

The fourth key factor is your <u>Competence</u>.

Where possible people will assess your compentence in advance using your track record. It follows that you need to regard your track record as a silent recommender (or off-putter!) If your track record is not available to people then they'll need to take you 'on faith', in which case they'll rely more on the other factors in judging whether or not to join you on your journey.

Once people perceive that you're going on a journey they'd like to be on too because they see it as adding value to their own life, and they believe that you have what it takes to get them there, they become candidates to join you. The next step is for you to invite them on your journey, or in some other way make it possible for them to sign up. Thus people can enrol with a feeling of wanting to join, rather than from a feeling of having to join.

While it may seem mechanical, the whole process of enrolment is a key step to getting people to help you accomplish the outcomes you want. This is the point at which people decide to commit their time, energy and resources to your cause.

Once people have joined you on your journey, it becomes their journey too. They become your partners, and will need to be treated as such. There are bound to be things along the way that your partners know more about than you do. It's important to let them take the lead for that part — it's the best way for you to make progress at that point, and they'll have a strong sense of personal contribution to the result.

Collectively, you and your partners represent what Napoleon Hill[3] describes as a 'master mind' in his classic book, *Think and Grow Rich*. With a master mind you can overcome obstacles and make progress faster and more effectively than if you tried to lead the entire journey yourself.

You can see that in enrolling people to help you reach your destination, you yourself are the limiting factor. It's your ability that counts, your ability to formulate and articulate a compelling vision, your ability to enrol others to assist, and your ability to lead others to accomplish the outcomes you want. Nobody else can do that for you — it's your responsibility, and it's your opportunity!

Maybe it goes without saying, but your vision is a beginning,
not an outcome. If your vision describes what you want to
accomplish, then accomplishing it is what really matters. In
the end, it's results that count. The vision itself, while critical to the process, is still just an energising and focusing
mechanism that helps you to direct your own energy and the
energy of others towards accomplishing the outcomes that
you want.

It's you and the people that you enrol in your vision who
provide the commitment and energy needed for the vision to
become reality. While the vision provides a focus for action,
it's the action that accomplishes the results.

What roles do you as the leader play in this action phase?
The first and most important role is to keep your vision
alive, for yourself and for the people that you've enrolled to
help you. You do this through your ongoing commitment to
your vision. There is no substitute for this commitment.

Either you're fully committed or you're not. It's that simple.

In our experience, your effectiveness in achieving the outcomes you want is directly related to your level of personal commitment. Thus, if you truly want some specific results, you must fully commit yourself to delivering them. Conversely, if you find yourself or others giving reasons why results haven't been or won't be achieved, you or they are probably not fully committed to delivering those results. In our experience, giving reasons instead of results is a very clear indicator of lack of commitment.

True commitment is not hard to maintain. You're fully committed and that's that. The bottom line is that if you're struggling to maintain your commitment, then you're not fully committed. If you're having any difficulty maintaining your commitment as time passes, we suggest you reread our comments about commitment in chapter three.

Your next key role as leader is to hand over your vision to the people you've enrolled to help you. Unfortunately, many would-be leaders still get this completely wrong. They set out to take all the decisions and solve all the problems, leaving their helpers to do all the work. Instead, you need to work with your helpers so that they can translate your vision into their own actions. They can then own and be responsible for their performance and their results.

Professors Warren Bennis and Burt Nanus[4] describe leadership this way:

'Leadership is a transaction between leaders and followers. [It's] an impressive and subtle sweeping back and forth of energy.'

How do you make sure you stay on course?

In this process, people are watching you closely, and they quite reasonably expect you to live your vision fully.

Your next role as a leader is to be an example to others. At this point leadership is more about action than words. How do you share your vision, handle mistakes, recover from failures, get results, tie in people's contributions, and adapt to changed circumstances? All of your behaviours in handling these events carry messages that can reinforce or dilute people's commitment to you and to helping you accomplish the outcomes you want.

People are very astute in observing the alignment, or lack of it, that you display between your words (vision) and your deeds (action) as time passes. Our view is that if you are truly committed your words and deeds are likely to be very closely aligned, and you'll be focused on results, not on reasons. In reverse, if your words and deeds aren't closely aligned, or if you're focusing on reasons rather than results, we suggest that it's time to check your commitment.

A very important part of demonstrating this alignment is keeping your word. In the end people are helping you based on your vision, which is your word. If you don't keep your word, even in little ways, this quickly damages your credibility and trustworthiness in the eyes of your people. You probably intuitively know this already because you feel that way yourself when others don't keep their word with you.

You might well see yourself as one who keeps their word, but do you? If you have children, do you live up to what you tell them you'll do? If you have customers, suppliers or employees, do you always do what you tell them you'll do? If you say you'll be somewhere or provide something at a certain date or time, do you always deliver? If not, do you always concede beforehand that you're not going to be able to keep your word, and agree on a new commitment?

Some of these things may not seem all that important to you as they happen, particularly if there are other 'bigger fish to fry' at the time. As you know from the times when you're on the receiving end of other people's non-delivery, they all count. Our advice is that if you're needing to lift your game in this area do it now, and stick with it. The rewards of doing so will accumulate over time.

Your next key role as a leader is to communicate, and most importantly, to keep communicating. A key aspect of keeping your word and making sure others keep theirs, is to communicate clearly. How often have you seen people take different meanings from the same communication? Maybe they're even unaware that they've done so! In our experience this is very common. The problem is it results in mistakes or misalignment, and it weakens your collective ability to accomplish the outcomes you intended. It can even result in you missing your target completely. Our advice? Focus on developing your ability to communicate precisely, and help your people to do this too.

Of course, even when communication is very precise, people can and do take different meanings from it. This is because they interpret it and react to it differently. For example, if people hear that it'll rain today, some will be unhappy because they hate getting wet, while others will be delighted because they love the sound and smell of rain and the good it does for the garden.

These different reactions also happen in response to

events, like the rain itself. Of course the rain is neither good nor bad, it simply is. Rain happened long before humans existed, and no doubt it will still happen even if humans are gone!

Your next key role as a leader is to handle unwanted events well. Many events will occur along your journey. In themselves these events are completely neutral, but the way that you in particular react to them will be key to your progress. Naturally, the events that you want are welcome! It's the unwanted ones that cause problems. A typical reaction to a neutral event that you interpret as unwanted is 'oh no!' followed by a negative cycle of resistance to the perceived 'problem'. In our experience, this is very damaging to your progress as it typically leads to indulging in one or several mind traps, for example 'worry', 'victim' or 'resentment'.

Why do people give this 'oh no!' response? In our view it's because they see the seeds of failure in unwanted events, and the prospect of failure threatens their striving for perfection. The result is that they have a fear of failure. This fear of failure leads them to 'play safe'. As time passes this playing safe limits their ability to handle unwanted events well. The problem is, handling unwanted events well is one of a leader's key roles, so leaders can't afford to be operating from a fear of failure.

What would be a better approach? In our experience the best alternative to operating from fear of failure is operating from learning and discovery. That way, when an unwanted event occurs, it's an opportunity to learn how to handle such events creatively. If you combine this approach with vision and true commitment, you'll be able to treat unwanted events as 'setbacks' instead of failures. You may end up taking a different path as a result, but because of your vision it'll be to the same destination, and because of your commitment you'll never give up.

When you're coming from discovery you can choose to react differently at the 'oh no!' point. The reality is that each event is neutral and, as always, you have a choice in how you react to it. When you're coming from discovery, instead of resisting the 'problem' at this point, you'll be looking for ways to make the best of the 'opportunity'.

Imagine that you're playing chess. Your opponent makes a good move. If you're a good player your reaction will be 'uh-huh'. You'll be able to see the new situation as though this was the point at which you entered the game. You'll have no regret about what's gone before, and you'll challenge yourself to find the most inspired winning move you can. With this attitude you're able to go on to 'ah ha!' and make a very good next move. By contrast, if your reaction to the other player's move is 'oh no!', you're focusing on the problem it presents you with, perhaps regretting some earlier weak move you made, and with all this in mind your next move is very unlikely to be the best it could be. As always, where your focus goes, your energy flows.

Your next key role as a leader is to step up to the things that need to be handled personally by the leader. What are those things? Our view is that a leader's personal focus is most needed on keeping their vision alive and well, and personally handling the most important problems and opportunities along the way. By definition these are the things that are tough, important, and central to achieving the outcomes you want. They need your personal attention because failing to address them effectively will probably result in your failing to accomplish the outcomes you want, and if you're truly committed, that's just not acceptable.

Your next key role as a leader is to set and keep priorities. People often over-complicate this, but in our view it's really very simple. As Stephen Covey[5] says in his best-selling book *First Things First*, 'the main thing is to keep the main thing the main thing.' This may seem obvious, but in our experience many people don't focus their personal energy this way. Do you?

> *Here's the test. List your three most important issues in accomplishing the outcomes you intend to create. Do that now, before you read on.*

Now, if you had an accurate diary record of how you spent your time, and then analysed it, would it show that you spent most of your time on those three issues and on keeping the vision alive and well? If not, then we recommend that you rethink how and where you spend your time.

We also suggest that you consider why you do it that way. Have you just not thought it through, or are you avoiding your key issues, and if so why? Let's face it, if you're not addressing these issues, who is? Your people? Why would they, when they can see that your own actions aren't committed to pursuing your own vision? The bottom line is that the biggest issues are yours to address, and you need to be the one who addresses them.

All these leadership roles are key to staying on course so

that you achieve the outcomes you want. There's also one crucial role that you play inside yourself, and that's persistence. When the going gets tough, when you need to dig deep, or when you need to go the extra mile, you persist, persist, persist. And as you'll know by now, the power of persistence comes directly from your commitment.

When I go back to my old ways, my wife says I need to go back and learn the principles of accomplishment again.
— M.

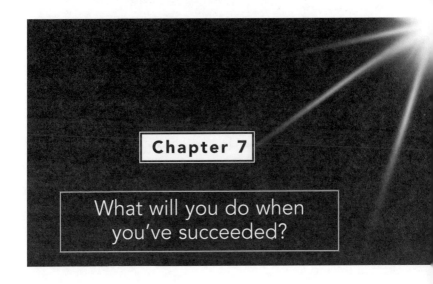

Chapter 7

What will you do when you've succeeded?

Will you know when you've accomplished the outcomes you want? Strange as that might sound, often there's no definite 'finish line' to tell you that you've arrived at the end of your journey. In fact, if you weren't 100 percent clear at the outset about the outcomes you wanted to accomplish, then your journey might not even have a definite end point. Even if you were clear at the outset, you might still have no definite way to confirm that you've arrived.

Let's look at some examples. Say the outcome you want is to become a published author. Here the finish line is very clear: book published — outcome achieved. But what if the outcome you want is to build a venture to develop people's leadership skills. When will you be able to say that you've accomplished that? At the end of the day, how many people is 'enough'?

The reality is, you get to a point when you feel that you've 'probably done it by now', or that you've 'more or less accomplished' what you set out to do. And the chances are that this is as close as you'll get to 'knowing for sure' that you're there at last. Is this true for you? If so, we heartily congratulate you, and we encourage you to acknowledge and celebrate what you've created. This, after all, is what your incredible journey has been all about!

In our experience, it's likely that by the time you get to this point, your vision has evolved further, so that 'the outcomes you want' are now more ambitious, and as a result the accomplishment of these further outcomes is still very much in the future.

Vision has a way of operating like that. It's larger than life, it's bigger than you are, and it keeps evolving as you move along your journey towards it. We see this as a very positive development, as long as you acknowledge and celebrate when you've accomplished the outcomes that you originally wanted. You don't want to end up like the proverbial donkey with a carrot dangling from a stick in front of it, never getting any closer as it moves forward.

Although it may seem that expanding your vision as you go is tougher than simply accomplishing the outcomes you originally wanted, people often find that the reverse is true. This is because life's a journey, and arriving means … what exactly? What now? An encore? Another journey? Rest? No more journeys?

The answers to these questions may not be at all obvious as you contemplate them. You may not even feel free to really consider these questions. For example, if you've led others to accomplish what they wanted too, there may be pressure from them for you to lead them on to greater heights. Or if you've given people something they value very highly, there may be pressure from them for more. If you've been publicly acknowledged for what you've accomplished, there may be pressure from the press or the public to continue or to go on to greater things. If you've set a new record in the process, there may be pressure to stay at the top.

If you're subjected to these pressures, and some of them can be very powerful and tug insistently at your ego, you're at risk of setting out afresh to accomplish something that's more about what others want than what you want. At this point, our red flag goes up, because this is not the way to fulfilling your purpose in life.

Our advice is to revisit the Principles of Accomplishment, particularly the first one, which is to decide clearly, specifically and positively what you want to accomplish, and the second one, which is to commit yourself wholeheartedly. We're not suggesting that you ignore others' wishes. But we are clear that your personal decision and commitment are so fundamental to accomplishing the outcomes you want that if you proceed on any other basis you're on the wrong foot before you even start.

These pressures reveal the downside of success — the need to perform and to keep performing, and the feeling of failure and the fear of losing face if you don't. This is not a sound basis on which to go forward. In our view, your next steps are better based on wanting to grow. Remember that if money or fame traps you, it's really you that's trapping yourself, as is always the case with mind traps.

This is a time to revisit your purpose, to expand or create a new vision for the next stage of your life, and to move on in keeping with who you really are and what you really want to accomplish with your life. Thus you've come full circle, and you're back at the point where the book began. The point is, everything in the book applies again to the next stage, and the next, and the next. Whether each cycle is part of your job, part of your career, part of your personal growth, or part of your social contribution, the Principles of Accomplishment are the same, and the mind traps are the same.

With this in mind, we encourage you to reread this book. There's a lot in it, and we're sure that the second time round you'll find some valuable insights that you didn't discover on your first reading. We also encourage you to practise what's in the book, and to teach others what you've discovered and what works for you.

This was the most powerful experience I've ever had. By hell, this was … something real, unbelievable. — M.

As you put this learning into practice as an operating philosophy, remember that 'If it's to be, it's up to me'. Simply put, this means 'I create my own reality'. We've seen many people do this, and in doing so they've resoundingly created their own success.

Now it's your turn. We wish you great success as you go forward on your personal journey of discovery.

Endnotes

1. Kenton, Susannah and Leslie. *The New Raw Energy.* Random House, London, 1994.

2. De Mello, quoted in Lopez, Isabel O. in Spears, Larry C. (Ed.) 'Reflections on Leadership.' John Wiley & Sons, Inc., New York, 1995.

3. Hill, Napoleon. *Think and Grow Rich.* Hawthorne Books, New York, 1996.

4. Bennis, Warren and Nanus, Burt. *Leaders: The Strategies for Taking Charge.* Harper & Row, New York, 1987.

5. Covey, Stephen R. and Merrill, Roger A. *First Things First.* Simon & Schuster, New York, 1994.

Brian Martin

Since he left England in 1955, Brian has made New Zealand his home. Over the years he has made his mark as a successful international CEO in the highly competitive apparel industry.

Soon after he 'retired' at 49, Brian established IAS Australasia to bring the principles of accomplishment to his fellow business people in New Zealand, Japan and the Asia-Pacific region. From his base in the hills of Albany north of Auckland, Brian has brought the IAS learning programmes to thousands of people around New Zealand and internationally in the last ten years.

While he is Chairman and CEO of IAS, Brian is also an active facilitator in many IAS programs. From this hands-on involvement he has been profoundly influenced by the outstanding results that the programme graduates and their companies have created for themselves.

At 60, Brian plans to devote the next decade to raising several million dollars to fund the delivery of the IAS leadership programmes to the children of New Zealand. His dream is to teach Kiwi kids how to become leaders of their own lives, and in doing so make New Zealand a better place for themselves and their children.

Brian is an Executive Member of the Japan/New Zealand Business Council and a Fellow of the New Zealand Institute of Management. In 1998 he was selected as an honoured member of the International Who's Who of Professionals.

Peter Loeffen

Pete became a graduate of the IAS Genesis programme in 1995. Inspired by what he learnt in the Genesis programme, he moved on from his career in corporate senior management to found his own company, Business Change Masters. He and his wife now help senior business managers to master the accelerating pace of change by capturing their greatest opportunities and resolving their greatest problems.

After Genesis, Pete consolidated his learning by writing a series of papers about leadership and management effectiveness that, together with the subsequent years of personal coaching and mentoring of the business people around him, have led to the writing of this book with Brian.

Pete lives on Auckland's North Shore with his wife and two children.